Children of the World
Singapore

For a free color catalog describing Gareth Stevens' list of high-quality children's books, call 1-800-341-3569 (USA) or 1-800-461-9120 (Canada).

For their help in the preparation of *Children of the World: Singapore*, the editors gratefully thank the Embassy of Singapore, Washington, D.C.; Raymond Yoong Yoon Thong, Goh Kok Beng, and Jesvinder Kaur, Social Defense and Community Relations Division, Ministry of Community Development, Singapore; the Singapore Tourist Promotion Board; and Ashvin Thambyhy.

Picture credits: p. 42 (both), TED H. FUNK/Third Coast © 1982; p. 44, HORIZON/Globe Press/Third Coast © 1990; p. 48 (flag illustration), © Flag Research Center; p. 48 (bottom), TED H. FUNK/Third Coast © 1982.

Library of Congress Cataloging-in-Publication Data

Wright, David K.
     Singapore / written by David K. Wright.
       p. cm. — (Children of the world)
     Summary: Presents the life of a ten-year-old boy and his family in Singapore, describing his home and school activities and discussing the history, geography, ethnic composition, languages, culture, and other aspects of his country.
     ISBN 0-8368-0255-1
     1. Singapore—Juvenile literature. 2. Children—Singapore—Juvenile literature. [1. Singapore. 2. Family life—Singapore.] I. Title. II. Series: Children of the world (Milwaukee, Wis.)
DS598.S7W72   1990
959.57—dc20   89-43196

A Gareth Stevens Children's Books edition

Edited, designed, and produced by
Gareth Stevens Children's Books
1555 North RiverCenter Drive, Suite 201
Milwaukee, Wisconsin 53212, USA

Series editor: Valerie Weber
Editors: Kelli Peduzzi, Valerie Weber
Research editors: Patricia Lantier, John D. Rateliff
Designer: Laurie Shock
Map design: Sheri Gibbs

Printed in the United States of America

2 3 4 5 6 7 8 9 97 96 95 94 93 92

Children of the World
Singapore

Text and Photography
by David K. Wright

Gareth Stevens Children's Books
MILWAUKEE

. . . a note about *Children of the World*:

The children of the world live in fishing towns, Arctic regions, and urban centers, on islands and in mountain valleys, on sheep ranches and fruit farms. This series follows one child in each country through the pattern of his or her life. Candid photographs show the children with their families, at school, at play, and in their communities. The text describes the dreams of the children and, often through their own words, tells how they see themselves and their lives.

Each book also explores events that are unique to the country in which the child lives, including festivals, religious ceremonies, and national holidays. The *Children of the World* series does more than tell about foreign countries. It introduces the children of each country and shows readers what it is like to be a child in that country.

Children of the World includes the following published and soon-to-be-published titles:

Australia	El Salvador	Japan	Spain
Belize	England	Jordan	Sweden
Bhutan	Finland	Malaysia	Tanzania
Bolivia	France	Mexico	Thailand
Brazil	Greece	Nepal	Turkey
Burkina Faso	Guatemala	New Zealand	USSR
Burma (Myanmar)	Honduras	Nicaragua	Vietnam
Canada	Hong Kong	Panama	West Germany
China	Hungary	Philippines	Yugoslavia
Costa Rica	India	Poland	Zambia
Cuba	Indonesia	Singapore	
Czechoslovakia	Ireland	South Africa	
Egypt	Italy	South Korea	

. . . and about *Singapore*:

Ten-year-old Harry Tan lives with his brother, sister, and parents in Ang Mo Kio, a suburb of Singapore City, the center of commerce and business in this bustling island nation. Harry goes sightseeing, runs errands with his father, and plays computer games, his favorite pastime. Harry is quiet and shy, but is very competitive and dreams of becoming a rich and powerful manufacturer.

To enhance this book's value in libraries and classrooms, comprehensive reference sections include up-to-date information about Singapore's geography, demographics, language, currency, education, culture, industry, and natural resources. *Singapore* also features a bibliography, research topics, activity projects, and discussions of such subjects as Singapore City, the country's history, language, political system, and ethnic and religious composition.

The living conditions and experiences of children in Singapore vary according to economic, environmental, and ethnic circumstances. The reference sections help bring to life for young readers the diversity and richness of the culture and heritage of Singapore. Of particular interest are discussions of Singapore's geography and its long and exciting history.

CONTENTS

Harry Tan and his family, from left: brother, Frank; sister, Wendy; Harry; mother, Margaret, and father, Patrick.

LIVING IN SINGAPORE:
Harry, a Modern Boy

Hello! My Name is Harry Tan.
嗨！您好，我是陈汉旸．

Meet 10-year-old Harry Tan, a boy from the island nation of Singapore. He lives with his parents, Patrick and Margaret, his 14-year-old brother, Frank, and his three-year-old sister, Wendy, in the suburb of Ang Mo Kio, north of central Singapore. The Tans also have a maid, Dina, a 22-year-old Filipino woman who has come to Singapore for two years to work and save money. The family dog is named Alaska.

Margaret comforts Alaska, the family dog, with Harry and Wendy.

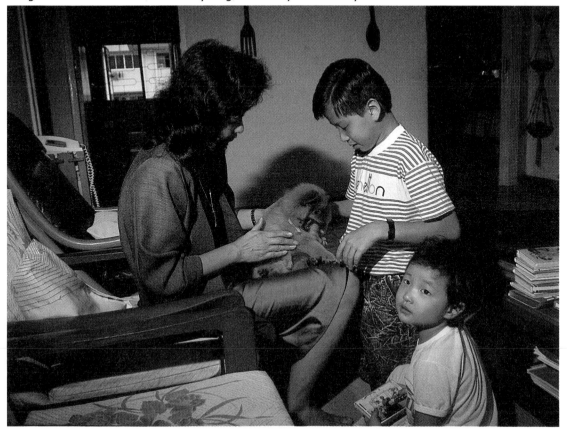

At Home with the Family

Harry's apartment is on the top floor of a ten-story building. If a breeze is blowing, the Tan family is sure to feel it that high up. The government, which builds 85% of the housing in Singapore, built the Tans' apartment. Housing is scarce, and people must wait as long as a year to buy an apartment in the suburb they want at the size they need. The Tan family moved here just before Harry was born.

The Tans' home is large by Singapore's standards. It has a big living-dining room, three bedrooms, a kitchen, and two baths. Harry's parents sleep in one bedroom with Wendy. Frank has his own room. Harry shares his bedroom with Dina. She sleeps on a bed that pulls out from beneath Harry's.

Mr. Tan has made several changes to the apartment. He covered the cement floors with cool tile. He put metal grill-work on the front door and on the windows. And he installed a doorbell that chirps like a songbird!

Harry and his family live in a large apartment on the top floor of this building.

Harry and Wendy with Dina, the family maid. Dina is from the Philippines. She does the family's cooking and cleaning and lives with the Tans. ▶

Modern appliances can be found in almost every room. The Tans have a VCR, a color television set, a telephone, a clothes washer, a stove, and a refrigerator. The Tans have a video camera, too. It is being repaired because the hot climate caused a fungus to grow inside it. They had a home computer, but the shop where it was being repaired burned down.

Harry has a video game system hooked to the TV set, plus many small, battery-powered computer games. Video games are his usual pastime. Harry plays them for hours, sometimes with his friends or Frank, and sometimes just by himself. He is quite competitive — he always wants to win.

Harry is shy and quiet, happy and stubborn. He answers questions quickly, with a nod or just a few words. "He's my most stubborn child, and he likes to argue," says his mother with a smile. She adds that his birthday is January 26, close to the Chinese New Year. That makes him lucky, she believes. She points to Harry's hair, where he has two identical curls, as another sign of luck. Harry rolls his eyes at his mother's superstition.

◀ Harry rides his skateboard outside his building.

Mr. Tan is self-employed as a builder. Building construction is one of the busiest trades in Singapore, and he has just finished building some condominiums. He has a portable telephone that he carries in his car and in the four-wheel-drive vehicle that he uses for work. He also brings the phone home for business calls.

Harry's father is a member of the local residence committee. Residence committees, which are common in Singapore, try to keep a friendly, villagelike feeling in government housing. They organize outings, set up arts and crafts and other classes, and make sure that buildings are clean and safe. "We want people to know and like and depend on their neighbors," Mr. Tan says.

Mr. Tan builds houses. He has a portable phone that works in or out of his car.

Mrs. Tan is a skilled tailor. Here she prepares cloth for cutting. ▶

Mrs. Tan is a tailor. She works six days a week, from 11:00 a.m. to 7:00 p.m. The shop where she works is famous for its beautiful dresses, made with expensive cloth that sometimes has gold or silver thread. Mrs. Tan went to school to learn her trade and is highly skilled. She saves her employer money by making the most of a piece of fabric. Mrs. Tan knows how to make good patterns that use little cloth yet fit the wearer well. She shows the seamstress who works with her how best to sew the patterns into a dress or shirt or blouse.

Frank is in the 8th grade and is very sports-minded. He is now at an age when he wants to spend all of his time with his friends. Harry and Frank argue and tease each other, but they stick up for each other in arguments with their mother. Little Wendy has not yet been to any school, but she has been to the United States. She went with her parents in 1988 on a visit to Mrs. Tan's brother and his family in New Jersey.

Harry wears T-shirts, jeans, and tennis shoes with famous labels. His bright clothes are usually made in Singapore for companies in Europe and North America. The entire family dresses casually but very well. Mrs. Tan knows what her family enjoys wearing, and her sewing skill helps her choose what looks good. Like many people in Asian countries, Harry removes his green and white sports shoes before entering his clean house. But he doesn't leave them on the apartment doorstep, where everyone else leaves shoes. Instead, he keeps them safely in a closet. He doesn't worry that someone will steal them, but he does want to keep them looking new.

Baseball is among Frank's favorite sports.

Harry, a skilled model builder, shows off the collection of models he has made. He requires only a little help from his dad. ▶

Traditional Singapore sights, such as this human-powered *trishaw*, are disappearing. Trishaws are being replaced by modern cars, taxis, and buses.

A traditional Buddhist temple on a Singapore street displays lots of red and gold. ▶

Mr. Tan points out that food and clothing are inexpensive, but homes and cars cost a bundle. A new car can easily cost $60,000 or more. That's because the government taxes cars heavily so that more people will use public buses and subways. Homes cost a lot because land is scarce.

The Tans are descended from people who were Buddhists and Taoists who worshiped their ancestors. But the Tan family is one of a growing number of Singaporeans who are secular — they don't practice any religion. "We believe our children should be free to choose a religion," says Mr. Tan. Although Harry attends a Catholic school, he says he does not think often of religion.

Singapore's skyline, as seen from the resort island of Sentosa.

Running Errands

Today is Saturday. Frank has gone camping with his friends for a few days at an oceanside chalet. Harry and his father run errands. They drop Mrs. Tan at the shop, pausing briefly to admire her tailoring work.

Harry and his dad stop at a corner restaurant for lunch. Mr. Tan orders for the two of them: pork with rice, flour puffs, soy sauce mixed with chili peppers, and tea. The tea stays hot on a small burner beside the table. Harry's father says this is typical Hokkien food, a type of cooking from the Hokkien area of mainland China.

Mr. Tan's side of the family came from the Hokkien area. Harry's grandfather, who lives near the Tans, was once a bodyguard for a warlord. Harry's father speaks to everyone in his or her native language: Hokkien Chinese to Mrs. Tan, Mandarin Chinese to his children, Malay or Tamil (an Indian language) to his workers, and English to visitors!

Harry often sees his grandfather, who lives near the Tans. ▶

Harry and Mr. Tan eat pork, rice, flour puffs, and spicy sauce, and drink tea.

Mrs. Tan also has an interesting history. One side of her family is Peranakan, or Baba. Babas are people of Chinese origin who lived for years in southwestern Malaysia, and who adopted Malay ways down through the years. Baba food, for instance, features Malay ingredients, such as coconut, in traditional Chinese dishes.

The next stop is the high point of Harry's day. They go to Mr. Tan's shooting club, where Harry's father looks over his 11 guns to make sure no rust has formed anywhere. He doesn't hunt animals. Instead, he prefers to shoot skeet, a type of shooting using flying clay targets. Mr. Tan is an excellent shot and has represented Singapore as a marksman in international games.

Harry sometimes gets to put on the protective earmuffs and fire the big magnum or some other handgun at a target. His father says he's a pretty good shot and encourages Harry to keep at it. Harry became a whiz at video games by playing for hours at a time, so he knows that practice pays off.

◀ After lunch, Harry and his dad check on a piece of Mr. Tan's construction equipment.

Harry and Wendy play a video game.

Harry's Favorite Time of Year

Winter is Harry's favorite time of the year. He has just begun his longest vacation from school. From mid-November until early January, he can do as he pleases.

Besides having seven weeks off in November and December, Harry is free for a week in the winter for the Chinese New Year, a week in the spring for Easter, and four weeks in June.

This vacation period is also Harry's favorite because the weather in this tiny island nation in Southeast Asia is a bit cooler. From March to November, the temperature is usually a scorching 90° to 95°F (32° to 35°C). But from mid-November to March, temperatures often drop below 85°F (29°C). A rain shower almost every winter day helps interrupt the heat.

Background: Coconut palms grow wherever they are planted on the lush, tropical island.

Harry aims for the basket at a community basketball court near his home.

Harry's School Days

When Harry returns to school after vacation, he will begin 5th grade. Harry attends Maris Stella School, a private Catholic school for boys. Even though the Catholic church runs the school, boys of many religions attend. The school year has 200 days, and Harry has to wear white shorts and a white shirt on every one. On Mondays, the boys must wear blue ties, too, in case special ceremonies are held. Harry is glad to be on vacation, when he can wear his casual clothes.

When school is in session, Harry must get up at 5:30 a.m. Monday through Friday. He gulps a cup of hot chocolate and sometimes eats a slice of bread for breakfast. After cleaning up, brushing his teeth, and dressing, he catches a public bus at 6:30. He rides for 45 minutes to school, which begins at 7:30. Students are ranked from A to F in Harry's school, with A's being the brightest. All of Harry's classes are in the A or B rank, and he studies hard. His favorite class is English. His other subjects are Chinese, social studies, mathematics, science, arts and crafts, and physical education.

During recess, at about 10:00 a.m., Harry buys rice with chicken in spicy curry gravy, plus a soft drink. School ends at 12:55 p.m., and he gets home at about 1:45 p.m. Even though Harry ate a good snack at school, he has a hearty appetite and looks forward to a big lunch. Dina fixes it for him unless Harry wants to cook. The dishes he makes most often are eggs, ham, and french fries.

Top: Harry in the courtyard of Maris Stella School.

Inset: Harry reads his English textbook. English is his favorite subject, and he speaks the language well.

Hand-held video games are a challenge.

Collecting rare or interesting coins from all over the world is one of Harry's hobbies. ▶

Sometimes, Harry avoids the midday heat with a short nap after lunch. Then he does schoolwork, plays with his sister, works on building a radio-controlled model car, checks his coin collection, or plays computer games. After a dinner of fish, vegetables, soup, rice, and eggs at about 7:30 p.m., it's cool enough to play outside. Frank and Harry sometimes play basketball or baseball on a lighted, paved court near their building. Like most people in Singapore, Harry makes the most of the cool evening hours, going to bed quite late at 11:00 p.m.!

Please do not touch

A Neighborhood School

While Harry enjoys his vacation, many children are in their final week of public school. At Kebun Baru Primary School, just two blocks from Harry's building, students stay busy so the time will pass quickly.

Some students create a social studies exhibit. Others practice a dance for an end-of-school assembly. Others take a music lesson. Still others clean the classroom, put displays and supplies away, or practice their English with the help of an overhead projector.

School lessons are all in English. Usually, students also study whatever language is spoken in their homes. Harry's neighbors, an Indian family, would see that their children learn Tamil. The children of Richard Smith, a friend of Mr. Tan's, would learn Malay. But more and more non-Chinese children are also learning to speak Chinese, the language of Singapore's majority.

◄ The students of Kebun Baru created paintings, Chinese masks, and other handicraft for their social studies exhibit.

Students at Kebun Baru listen carefully to a lesson. Much of Singapore's population is young, and public schools are crowded.

Each class at Kebun Baru lasts for 30 minutes. The school, which was built in 1962, is crowded. Nine hundred children attend from 7:30 a.m. to 1:00 p.m., and 900 others attend from 1:00 p.m. to 6:15 p.m., Monday through Friday. They also come to school for clubs, games, and other activities for two hours each Saturday morning. Teachers are required to teach at least one of these Saturday-morning activities each week, for which they receive an extra month's pay.

No one in Singapore is forced to attend school, but everyone does. School has become more and more important, since both parents usually work all day, away from home. Some mothers who live nearby come to school to have lunch with their children. They buy food from the school stalls and are welcomed each day by the teachers and children. Mothers and fathers are very interested in the future of their children.

Teachers try to make school a pleasant place, because there is so much pressure on even the youngest students to do well. Exams are given twice a year, with the most important tests given in 3rd grade and in 6th grade. These tests last four days each! How children do on these tests can affect their later lives. Harry takes his big exam in two years. He's not worried, though, because he's a good student.

A teacher carries tea in the cafeteria at Kebun Baru Primary School.

A corner of the cafeteria displays books that the children can buy. ▶

Family Vacations

The Tans take several vacations each year. They usually go to Malaysia, which is just across a bridge to the mainland of Asia. Many of their favorite vacation areas in Malaysia are just a brief drive for the family. In fact, Singaporeans go to Malaysia so often that they have a special passport just for that country.

Once in Malaysia, the Tans play golf, swim, jog, hike, see the sights, and relax. Harry really enjoys swimming. On weekends, Mr. Tan sometimes drives to Malaysia for a game of golf. It's less expensive and less crowded than in Singapore.

The Tans usually also go to Malaysia for Chinese New Year, which is in January or February each year. They leave Singapore to see the New Year fireworks, because although fireworks have always been a part of the holiday, Singapore no longer allows them. But Malaysia has relaxed its laws enough to allow fireworks at this special time of year. Chinese New Year is the most festive holiday in Singapore. Families come from far away to see each other, stores close, and there's lots to eat.

Inset: The rugged terrain near Malaysia's border with Thailand.

The beach of Penang Island in Malaysia.

Harry Goes Sightseeing

It's Sunday morning, and Harry has planned to go sightseeing. He decides to take an adult friend to visit one of Harry's favorite places, Sentosa Island, where he goes at least once a year. Sentosa is a resort island near Singapore's central city. It has a lot to offer a boy like Harry, who is curious about anything new.

Before he goes, Harry's mother shops for food. Later, she will play *mahjong,* a game similar to dominoes, with friends and relatives. Mr. Tan will play golf or go to the shooting range. Mrs. Tan soon returns with breakfast treats that are Baba specialties.

One is carrot cake, a rich, flat, fried cake with a seafood flavor. Another is red tortoise cake, which is sweetened green-bean paste inside a shell made of dyed rice flour. Other treats include bean curd and noodles. Harry has a bowl of cereal and samples the Baba food.

After breakfast, Harry catches a bus. A short ride brings him to the subway station. The subway is like many other things in Singapore — new, clean, and air-conditioned. After a long subway ride and a short taxi ride, Harry arrives at the ferry dock. High in the air above him, Harry sees the cable cars that travel from one of Singapore's highest hills to Sentosa Island. Harry has heard his father tell of a passing ship hitting the cable. He decides to play it safe and take the passenger ferry!

This is the view ferryboat passengers get as they arrive at Sentosa, Singapore's resort island. ▶

Cable cars carry passengers from Singapore to Sentosa Island.

Sentosa is much like the rest of Singapore: beautifully landscaped, very clean, and either new or freshly painted. But unlike the main island, not many people are there. Harry wanders from one attraction to the next, concentrating on each new sight — he doesn't want to miss a thing.

The day is very hot. Luckily, most attractions are just a short walk from each other, because Harry wants to see them all — a beautiful beach, a monorail, a rock museum, lovely gardens, a roller-skating rink, historic buildings where British soldiers once lived, and more. Harry studies the rock exhibit for a long time. A morning of sightseeing makes Harry hungry — for fast food. Fast-food chains are everywhere in Singapore. Harry has a cheeseburger and a soft drink and pronounces both "delicious."

Minutes later, after the return ferry ride, Harry is back in Singapore's central city for more sightseeing. Although he doesn't come to the central city often, he likes the crowds and the sights. Harry heads for his favorite toy store, where he checks out the latest model cars. Passing a toy globe, he gives it a spin and quickly finds his home.

◀ Like everywhere else in Singapore, Sentosa is lush and green.

◀ Inset: Singapore's beaches are pretty and seldom crowded.

This Singapore handicraft store sells Malay-style baskets and mats.

Above: A typical boat quay on the Singapore River.

Left: A merchant transports his bananas by bicycle cart in downtown Singapore.

Rain showers slow traffic almost every day. ▶

Harry's stroll through the city is cut short by a rain shower. Huge gray clouds blot out the sun, and thunder booms in the hot, still air. Fat raindrops fall fast, flooding curbs and gutters. Pedestrians stand under awnings and inside air-conditioned buildings. Harry runs for shelter, too. The end of the storm brings a cooler breeze.

Hopping aboard the subway and a bus once again, Harry is home in 30 minutes. He has his own mailbox key, but since it's Sunday, he won't check the box until Monday. He rides the elevator up to his home. Harry is wearing his new pair of running shoes. Like everyone else who comes to his front door, he takes off his shoes before entering. But he never leaves them outside.

Keeping Arts and Crafts Alive at Rasa Singapura

Singapore is a modern place in every sense of the word. Nevertheless, residents make efforts to keep traditional arts and crafts alive. Ancient skills survive at Rasa Singapura, a place set aside near the central city for artists, craftspeople, and hawkers of everything from exotic food to oil paintings.

Many of these people once sold their wares from rickety old pushcarts. But nowadays, streets are too thick and dangerous with traffic. So the vendors work out of stalls that are popular places for residents and tourists to meet after dark. After looking at all the handicraft and tasty food, visitors sometimes see Indonesian dancers or Malay orchestras perform at Rasa Singapura.

Harry will probably never hammer tin or set a stone, but he appreciates the artists who maintain the ancient skills. The time he spends carefully building scale-model airplanes and cars helps him understand their great skill.

A Chinese opera star.

A shopkeeper carefully letters a sign with Chinese characters. ▶

Harry's Ambition

Harry wants to do well in school because he has big plans. He says he wants to be a manufacturer. Harry has learned in school about Singaporeans who made things and sold them all over the world. Their industriousness has given the small nation a high standard of living where everything is new and works well, and he wants to be just like them.

Will Harry become rich? He is quiet, but he does well in school and is quite competitive. He can hold his own in arguments with his brother and he is very independent. He loves to tease his sister and his little dog, Alaska, yet he is really polite and kind. Harry dreams of the ambitious future he has planned and wonders if he has what it takes to be a powerful and important adult in the 21st century.

◀ Harry and Alaska are the best of friends.

FOR YOUR INFORMATION: Singapore

Official Name: Republic of Singapore (SING-uh-pore)

Capital: Singapore

History

The First Settlers

For centuries before a formal ruler governed, the island of Singapore was not a pleasant place to live. It was swampy and hot. The large island and its more than 50 small outlying islands were good hiding places for deadly pirates. The land was not good for farming, either. The earliest settlers were probably Malay or Indonesian farmers and fishermen from Asia and nearby islands. They arrived to find the inhospitable land swarming with mosquitoes. Even worse, these insects passed on malaria, a tropical disease caused by blood parasites, to the humans.

Memorial Park overlooks Singapore's busy harbor.

Nila Utama was the first recorded ruler of Singapore. He was a prince from the large island of Sumatra, to the southwest. Ancient records say he moved his kingdom to Singapore in AD 1299. The island's small port city was then called Temasek, but Prince Utama changed it to Singa Pur, Sanskrit for "city of the lion," because he thought he had seen a lion when he arrived.

Because Singapore was on the sea route halfway between India and China, two large trading markets, trade became brisk in Singapore. Wealthy merchants and rulers could afford to build lavish homes on the island's highest hill. They forbade others to come near them, so the place became known as Bukit Larangan, or Forbidden Hill.

In the 14th century, the kingdom was attacked and wiped out by a powerful army from the island of Java, to the southeast. Most of the population was killed, and the great trading city collapsed. For about 500 years afterward, Singapore's only residents were a few small bands of seafaring nomads. They anchored their boats in the many rivers and creeks, and only small-scale trading took place.

Singapore began to come to life again as the 19th century began. A Malayan sultan, Temenggong Abdul Rahman, moved to Singapore with 150 followers. He established a settlement on the bank of the Singapore River. At about the same time, Chinese farmers began to settle in Singapore. They carved large plantations out of the heavily forested interior.

The British Arrive

On January 28, 1819, Sir Thomas Stamford Raffles of Great Britain sailed into the Singapore River from the South China Sea. He immediately saw Singapore's advantages as a trading location, and he set up a trading post for Britain's East India Company. In 1824, Raffles made an agreement with the sultan of Johore, who ruled Singapore. The agreement allowed Great Britain to rent the island in perpetuity, or forever. This gave Great Britain a permanent trading post in the region.

Britain also had trading posts in China, and it established a busy trading route between the two countries. Chinese *junks*, flat-bottomed boats, sailed into Singapore's port to unload and pick up goods for the return trip. They came each year from January to March, pushed along by the northeast *monsoon*, the great wind. They brought porcelain, silk, and news from home to the island's many recent Chinese settlers. They returned to China with British and Indian goods.

From September to November each year, Bugi ships crowded the harbor. The Bugis were great sailors from Indonesia, guided to Singapore by winds from the southeast. They brought spices, tortoise shells, sea cucumbers, birds' nests, and other jungle products. They traded these for tobacco, silk, china, brass, and more, which they took back to Indonesia.

One of Singapore's major exports was a plant called *gambier*. The leaves of the gambier plant were boiled and used to dye cloth. The demand for the dye was huge. Hundreds of Chinese came to harvest gambier on large plantations. The work was hot and difficult, and the hours were long.

A City on the Rise

Singapore's bustling port became a major city. By 1830, its population had reached 10,000. To house all these new people, land was reclaimed from swamps and sea, and buildings went up. One of these reclaimed areas was Commercial Square, which soon became the financial center of Southeast Asia. The square was renamed Raffles Place in 1858, after Sir Thomas Stamford Raffles. To this day, Raffles Place remains the business center of the island.

Not everyone who worked in Singapore was rich. The need for new buildings was so great that in the 1860s, the British brought convicted criminals from India and put them to work as bricklayers, brick and tile makers, blacksmiths, plumbers, and stonecutters. The Indian workers made sturdy buildings, but the British didn't pay them for their hard labor. The British grew rich off the free convict labor, but if their sentences ran out while they were in Singapore, the convicts could go free. Many freed convicts thus found jobs and settled down permanently in Singapore.

Most Chinese immigrants were "coolies," or hired laborers. Their needs were ignored by the British, so they formed clans and associations, just as they had done in China. Leaders of such groups settled arguments in the Chinese community and acted as go-betweens for the British government and for the immigrants.

The Housing Shortage

By 1900, housing had failed to keep pace with the growing population. Rooms were divided into dozens of sleeping spaces and rented for lots of money. Diseases spread easily in these crowded conditions and crime increased, especially in terribly crowded Chinatown. Not until 1927 did Singapore start a public housing program, and then it was only for middle-class residents. The poor continued to live in small rooms.

To head off the rise of social problems, Indian and Chinese community leaders encouraged women to immigrate. The leaders thought that men with families would be less likely to fight, gamble, or abuse alcohol and other drugs. Terrible economic conditions in China and India made immigration attractive to women, and many moved to Singapore. Housing grew even more scarce.

World War II

The British were content to govern Singapore with just a few people in charge of the entire island. But they also made the island one of Britain's main naval bases, and began to build forts, gun batteries, docks, and repair facilities for its naval forces. They called Singapore "The Gibraltar of the East," after the great British fortress on the tip of Spain, the Rock of Gibraltar. Then, when World War II began in Europe in 1939, most British ships returned to protect Britain. Only a small British military force remained behind to guard the island.

The first Japanese bomb fell on Singapore on December 8, 1941, the day after the Japanese bombed Pearl Harbor, Hawaii. The small British force aimed its guns toward the sea, awaiting the landing of thousands of Japanese troops. But the Japanese landed in Malaya and attacked Singapore from the mainland, surprising and overpowering the British. Many British soldiers were put into prisoner-of-war camps. The Japanese held a victory parade in Singapore on February 16, 1942.

The activities of the Chinese in Singapore were carefully checked by the victorious Japanese. Those who had joined in any anti-Japanese activities were taken away and never seen again. The Chinese who passed the examination had their foreheads, arms, or shirts stamped to show that they were not suspected of spying. Some spent a few months carefully preserving the stamps so that they would not be arrested!

After the war, the British returned to their colony. By this time, the city of Singapore had a million people, and it was still growing. It was finally given a royal charter, or legal status as a city. The City Day Celebration on September 22, 1951, featured 300 floats, including a water dragon that breathed fire as it crossed the harbor.

Under continuing British rule, a small number of people were becoming rich while progress in housing, education, wages, and employment lagged. Not everyone was content. On May 12, 1955, a group of students and workers called Communists staged a bloody riot to protest the poor living conditions. They agreed with Communists in mainland China that the island's wealth and property should be shared among all its people. Those who ran Singapore thought otherwise. The fighting resulted in death for two policemen, a student, and a reporter.

Independent at Last

The British promised Singapore independence in 1956 and lived up to their word in 1959. A Singaporean named Lee Kuan Yew formed the People's Action party (PAP), and became prime minister in 1959. He worked to join Singapore with Malaya to create the new Federation of Malaysia in 1963.

Almost immediately, the Malays were unhappy with Singapore's presence in the federation. They were afraid that the existence of a slight majority of ethnic Chinese would lead to discrimination against persons of Malay descent. Rather than agree to give the minority of Malays any kind of special treatment, as Malaya demanded, Singapore withdrew from the federation and became an independent republic in 1965.

Meanwhile, the Singapore economy had started to grow. People of any race or religion who were willing to work came to Singapore by the thousands. There, they found better housing, higher-paying jobs, and better schools and government welfare programs than those where they had lived before. The new immigrants loved Singapore, and Prime Minister Lee became so popular that he continues to rule today without any opposition.

Today, Singaporeans enjoy the highest standard of living in Southeast Asia. Some laws and rules are very harsh, however — a resident who fails to flush a public toilet can be fined hundreds of dollars! This is because Prime Minister Lee is a very tidy person and imposes his tidiness on the entire country. Large fines and even jail sentences are given for littering or other unsanitary actions. Lee's ruling party also censors magazines and newspapers that are critical of his government. But the country is clean and safe, despite long-standing rivalries among Malaysians, Chinese, and Indians.

Government

Singapore is a republic with a parliamentary form of government. Adult citizens are required by law to vote for members of Parliament. The Parliament passes laws and elects the president, whose job is mostly ceremonial. The real power lies with the prime minister, the leader of the party that holds the most seats in Parliament. So far, the most popular party has been Prime Minister Lee's People's Action party. Lee and his cabinet are the most powerful people in the government. The cabinet is in charge of everything from communications to defense, and its members meet with Lee to make decisions on all important issues.

The PAP has been in power since 1959. Much of its success has been because members were honest and worked hard, and they helped Singapore become a prosperous nation. Voters became such great PAP supporters that the only other party, the Socialist Front, dissolved in 1966. In 1981, however, a member of Singapore's Workers' party was elected to Parliament. This happened again in 1984. That was big news because no one but members of the People's Action party had been elected to Parliament since 1963!

Because of the country's small size, no major divisions exist between federal and local governments in Singapore's many small towns. National and local officials meet with each other frequently to solve problems.

The judicial system has several different levels of courts, however. Singapore's legal system is based on British common law, which relies on previous court decisions in deciding new cases. As with British law, appeals for new hearings can sometimes be made to the Judicial Committee of the Privy Council in London.

Drug possession and drug dealing are handled severely by police and courts in Singapore, where drug addiction is common. Most addicts smoke heroin, a strong painkiller. The heroin is made in Thailand, Burma, or Laos and then smuggled into Singapore. Singapore is one of the few places on earth where the drug problem is decreasing, however. Some believe that this is due to the harsh punishments that discourage people from buying, using, or selling drugs. The most severe punishment is the death penalty, given to drug dealers. By 1990, 25 convicted drug traffickers had been hanged. Others think that the country's efforts to treat its 9,000 drug addicts have helped reduce its addiction rate, too.

Education

Education is not compulsory. But Singaporean parents value it highly, so almost 100% of the children go to school. Following two years of kindergarten, children attend six years of primary school and four years of secondary school.

After secondary school, many young people go into the work force. Others attend two years of junior college. Following junior college or two years of work, young men must serve in the military for two years. Women, as well as men who have completed military service, can go to a four-year college at home or abroad.

Educational standards are high. Classes are crowded, with a typical classroom containing 40 students. Slower learners can take as many as eight years to finish primary school. Teachers have no patience with students who misbehave.

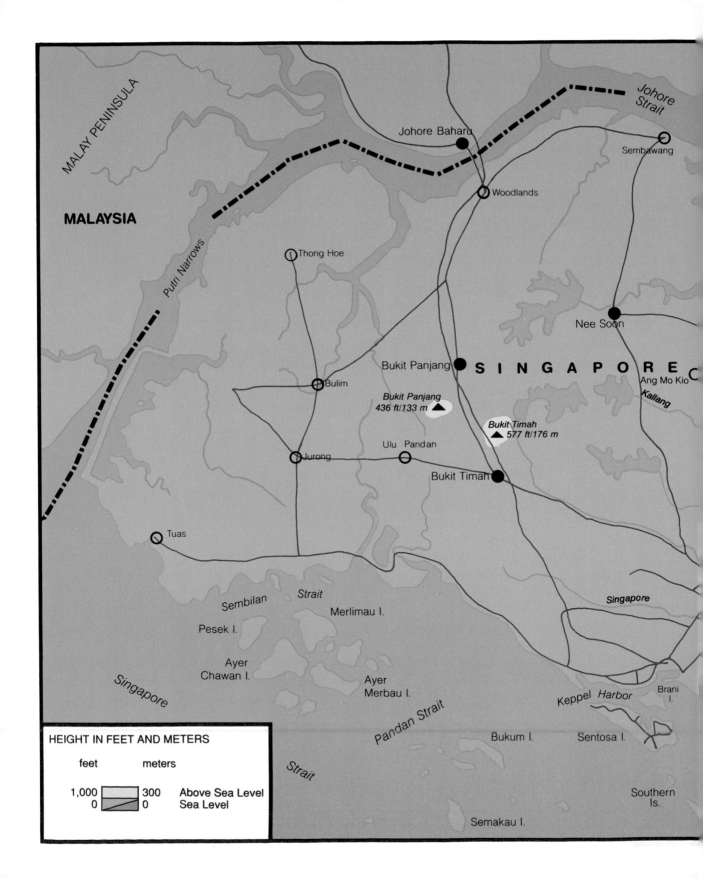

MALAY PENINSULA

Johore
Strait

Johore Baharu

Sembawang

MALAYSIA

Putri Narrows

Woodlands

Thong Hoe

Nee Soon

Bukit Panjang

Bukit Panjang
436 ft/133 m

S I N G A P O R E

Bulim

Ang Mo Kio

Kallang

Bukit Timah
577 ft/176 m

Ulu Pandan

Jurong

Bukit Timah

Tuas

Singapore

Sembilan
Strait

Merlimau I.

Pesek I.

Ayer
Chawan I.

Ayer
Merbau I.

Keppel Harbor

Brani
I.

Singapore

Pandan Strait

Bukum I.

Sentosa I.

Strait

Southern
Is.

Semakau I.

HEIGHT IN FEET AND METERS

feet   meters

1,000   300   Above Sea Level
0   0   Sea Level

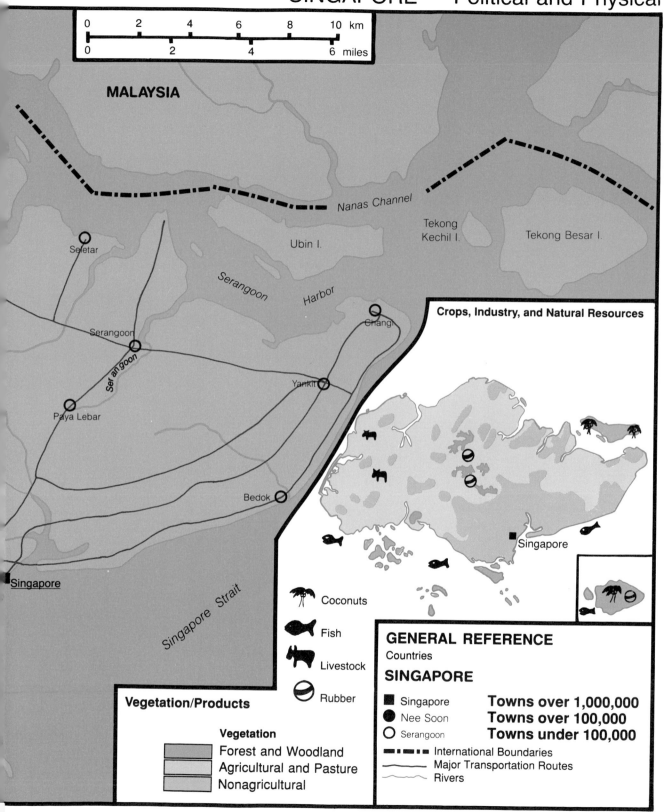

MALAYSIA

0 2 4 6 8 10 km
0 2 4 6 miles

Seletar

Nanas Channel

Ubin I.

Tekong Kechil I.

Tekong Besar I.

Serangoon Harbor

Changi

Serangoon

Serangoon

Yanklr

Paya Lebar

Bedok

Singapore

Singapore Strait

Crops, Industry, and Natural Resources

Singapore

Vegetation/Products

Coconuts

Fish

Livestock

Rubber

Vegetation

Forest and Woodland
Agricultural and Pasture
Nonagricultural

GENERAL REFERENCE

Countries

SINGAPORE

■ Singapore   **Towns over 1,000,000**
● Nee Soon   **Towns over 100,000**
○ Serangoon   **Towns under 100,000**

▬·▬·▬ International Boundaries
───── Major Transportation Routes
───── Rivers

Land and Climate

Singapore's main island is a tribute to good land management. Singaporeans have turned a swampy, low-lying, and hostile environment into a showplace. In doing so, they have created a nation in miniature, with everything they need in a very small area. The land is extremely flat. The highest point, Bukit Timah (Tin Hill), is just 577 feet (176 m) above sea level. The longest river runs only nine miles (14 km). The big urban area of Singapore was built on the south side of the island on land reclaimed from swamp and sea.

The main island is shaped roughly like a diamond and measures 14 miles (23 km) north to south and 26 miles (42 km) east to west. The total land area is 238 square miles (616 sq km), smaller than the state of Rhode Island or Canada's Prince Edward Island. This area includes over 50 nearby islets, few of which are populated.

The land lacks many soil nutrients. Yet orchids grow well enough to be an export, and vegetables are cultivated year-round for local kitchens. Rice is the staple food of Singapore, but it has to be imported from neighboring countries, such as Malaysia and Indonesia.

Being about 70 miles (110 km) north of the equator means that the heat is always on. High temperatures vary from 80° to above 90°F (27° to 32°C). But because there is always a breeze, record highs do not exceed 95°F (35°C). The only place where it is cool enough to wear a sweater is in some of the air-conditioned buildings!

Average annual rainfall totals 95 inches (241 cm) and falls as quick, heavy showers at all times of the year.

Located off the southern tip of the Malay Peninsula in Southeast Asia, Singapore is separated from the country of Malaysia, to the north, by a wide channel called the Johore Strait. To the southwest is the Indonesian island of Sumatra. The Indonesian island of Java lies to the southeast, and to the east lies Borneo, a huge island shared by Malaysia, Indonesia, and Brunei.

Industry and Natural Resources

Singapore is almost without natural resources. It makes up for its lack of coal, gold, or oil by being a processor of every kind of raw material found in the region. Raw materials processed here include rubber and tin from Malaysia, coffee from the island of Java, plus spices, foods, copra (the dried kernel of the coconut), and rattan (a plant used in weaving), from several different countries.

The work force totals 1.2 million people who are young, healthy, and well educated. Whenever there is full employment of native Singaporeans, foreigners are also allowed to work in Singapore. They are attracted by pay that is higher than most other places in Southeast Asia.

Manufacturing has grown steadily as Singapore has become a large banking center. This is because the banks loan money to Singaporeans who want to build factories. The largest single industry is petroleum refining. It is followed by electronics, transportation equipment, ship repair, textiles, electrical machinery, and food industries.

The demand for housing is high, and the building trades are always busy. The government is one of the largest builders, with 17 of every 20 citizens living in government housing. Older and smaller apartments are being torn down and newer and larger apartments are being built on the same spot as people have more money to spend on larger homes. With as many as three million tourists from all over the world coming to visit Singapore each year, hotel builders are also busy.

Singapore is becoming a big producer of high-technology goods. Countries such as Japan and the United States are beginning to take notice of Singapore's economic strength. They are worried that people will buy more goods from Singapore than from their countries.

Population and Ethnic Groups

Singapore is a "melting pot" where the cultures of China, India, and Malaysia meet. This mixture has created a society in which racial and ethnic loyalties have often resulted in clashes among the groups. The Chinese, who make up about 76% of Singapore's population, discovered when they emigrated from many areas of China that there were ethnic differences even among the people of their native land. To complicate matters, Peranakan or Baba Chinese from the Strait of Malacca were long-time residents of Malaysia who had adopted Malay ways but looked Chinese and spoke a Chinese language.

About 15% of the population is of Malay descent and has traditionally been rural. Indians, who make up 7% of the people, are from southern India or Sri Lanka, and many are descended from convicts or laborers.

Most residents see themselves as Singaporeans first and Chinese, Malay, or Indian second, but each group carefully maintains its own ethnic identity.

Currency

The Singapore dollar is worth about 53 cents in the United States and 60 cents in Canada. Coins include 10-, 20-, and 50-cent pieces. The smallest coin in use is the 5-cent piece. Commonly used bills include 1-, 5-, 10-, 20-, 50-, and 100-dollar notes. Paper money bears a watermark of Singapore's symbol, the merlion — half fish, half lion.

A Singaporean one-dollar bill.

Languages

English, depending on your point of view, is either everybody's or nobody's language in Singapore. It is promoted as the language of business and is spoken almost everywhere in public. Ideally, residents always speak English on the street and their own traditional language at home.

To make matters even more complicated, the Chinese have many dialects, or variations, of their language. To reduce confusion, they are encouraged to speak only Mandarin Chinese, the dialect spoken by the majority of people in China. Singapore's Malays speak Malay in the home, and the country's Indians most often speak Tamil. Therefore, four official languages exist in this tiny nation — English, Mandarin, Malay, and Tamil!

Religion

A growing number of people in Singapore — about 30% — have no religious preference. The Chinese are usually Buddhist, the Malays Muslim, and the Indians Hindu. Christians and Jews are few in number. The government endorses freedom of worship.

Buddhism is a religion without scheduled temple services. If a follower is passing a Buddhist temple, he or she may enter and burn incense to remember ancestors. Many Buddhist ceremonies are connected to holidays or superstitions or the need for good luck. The goal of this religion is to achieve enlighten-ment, free from worldly cares.

The Muslim faith is practiced by most Malays and some Indians. Loudspeakers remind Muslims to come to the mosque, or Muslim temple, for prayer five times each day. Known as Islam, the Muslim religion has simple rules for obeying Allah (God), and paying respect to Muhammad, known as the Prophet, who first proclaimed Allah's message in Arabia in the early 7th century AD.

Hinduism, which is followed by most Indians, teaches belief in reincarnation, where one's spirit is reborn into animals, other people, plants, and even nonliving things. This is why Hindus believe that some animals are sacred and why they are strict vegetarians.

Arts and Crafts

No arts or crafts are unique to Singapore. But all of the major ethnic groups brought their art forms with them to this small, steamy island. The Chinese love gold, jewelry, and precious stones. It's safe to say that there are probably more jewelry stores per person here than anywhere else on earth.

The gold most often seen in Singapore is 18- or 24-carat. That means that it is heavier, softer, and brighter than the gold seen in many other countries, and thus more valuable. Many of the stores selling gold are owned by persons of Indian heritage. They are skilled goldsmiths, turning the yellow lumps of metal into thin, beautiful necklaces and other kinds of jewelry.

Also found in many jewelry stores is jade, which the Chinese regard as the most precious of all stones. This stone, which is usually mined in Myanmar (formerly Burma) or China, is often carved into small statues and also made into bowls, vases, tablets, and jewelry. One of the world's great jade collections can be found in Singapore's National Museum and Art Gallery.

Singaporeans of Malaysian or Indonesian descent make *batik*. Batik is a method of decorating cloth using hot wax and various colorful dyes. Shirts, skirts, and bathing suits made in batik are quite popular.

The most beautiful buildings in Singapore are the houses of worship. Buddhist temples appear on fire with red and gold color. Hindu temples are covered with hand-painted statues, and Muslim mosques feature domes covered with intricate geometric patterns.

Sports and Recreation

Schoolchildren learn to play many different sports. The hope is that each student will find some sport to enjoy for the rest of his or her life. Surrounded by the sea, it makes sense that the country's most popular sport is swimming. Other popular sports include badminton, which can be played with or without a net, soccer, rugby, volleyball, table tennis, gymnastics, softball, and basketball. Basketball hoops and paved areas for roller skating can be found near most high-rise apartment buildings.

Adults are allowed to gamble on horse races. Older adults, especially those of Chinese descent, love to play table games, such as cards or *mahjong*, an ancient game using small tiles.

Singapore City

Singapore City is the nation's capital and its largest city. Despite its tiny size, the city does not feel crowded. That is due to careful planning by the government. High-rise apartment complexes are surrounded by parks, and every slope and hill that won't hold a building is planted with trees and flowers.

Singapore has been called "Instant Asia," because one can find something here from every corner of that vast continent. But what the visitor has a hard time finding in this city of more than 2.3 million people is the centuries-old mystery of the Far East.

Why? Because Singapore is so clean and modern! For every ancient, robed Buddhist monk, there are one hundred bankers in business suits. For every artisan shaping gold by hand, there are a dozen air-conditioned stores selling cheap Taiwanese copies of Swiss watches. For every elderly Chinese trishaw (three-wheeled rickshaw) driver, there are several Boeing 747 jets parked at the new Changi Airport.

The government wants to preserve the few remaining exotic streets even as it continues to approve plans for skyscrapers. But preserving old places is hard to do because the land is becoming more rare and valuable, so fewer and fewer old buildings survive. Singapore is one of the cleanest, safest, and wealthiest cities in the Far East, although this can sometimes seem dull to visitors who expect to see more of the old, exotic ways.

Singaporeans in North America

Except for a few hundred students who arrive each year, there are hardly any Singaporeans in the United States or Canada. This is mainly because there are so few residents of Singapore to begin with — only about 2.6 million. A small number of persons who were born in China may have spent a few early years in Singapore, but they now consider themselves US or Canadian residents of Chinese descent. Most Singaporean students who leave their country to study choose to go to Great Britain or Australia rather than come to North America.

Glossary of Mandarin Terms

boo syeh (boo SHAY) ....you're welcome
dzai jyen (zi YEN) ....good-bye
dzau (ZOW) ....good morning
ni how mah (nee how MAH)..............how are you?
xie xie ni (shay shay NEE) ....thank you

More Books about Singapore

The Fall of Singapore. Stein (Childrens Press)
Singapore. Wee (Chelsea House)
Take a Trip to Singapore. Elder (Franklin Watts)
We Live in Malaysia and Singapore. (Franklin Watts)

Things to Do — Research Projects

Singapore is a country made up of many different ethnic groups. It is home to people of Malaysian, Indian, and Chinese descent. Chinese make up the majority, yet many differences can be found among them as well. In the past, strife has sometimes erupted among the different ethnic groups in Singapore, and they have worked to keep their separate identities. But even though they are separated by race, language, religion, and culture, they have worked together to make a single nation.

As you read about Singapore, keep in mind the importance of having current facts. Some of the research projects that follow require accurate, up-to-date information. Two publications in your library will tell you about recent articles on many topics:

Readers' Guide to Periodical Literature
Children's Magazine Guide

Look up *Singapore* in these two publications. They will lead you to the most up-to-date information you can find.

1. Singapore is one of the few places in the world where one large city and its suburbs make up the whole country. Compare Singapore to the British Crown Colony of Hong Kong, off the southeastern tip of mainland China. What do these small but wealthy states have in common? Compare their histories, industries, and ethnic makeups. Find out why many people are starting to call Singapore "the new Hong Kong."

2. Because Singapore is located so close to the equator, its climate is quite different from that of North America. Instead of summer and winter, it has a wet season and a dry season. Find out what happens during these two seasons. What happens during a monsoon? How does the weather affect the lives of people in Singapore?

More Things to Do — Activities

1. Singapore is quickly becoming one of the world's top manufacturing centers, exporting goods all over the world. Find out what goods are made in Singapore. Check carefully at department stores in your area. Did you find any things marked "Made in Singapore"? Can you find any in your own home? Make a list of the goods you find. Are there any surprises on your list?

2. If you would like to have a pen pal from Singapore, write to these organizations:

International Pen Friends
P.O. Box 290065
Brooklyn, NY 11229

Worldwide Pen Friends
P.O. Box 39097
Downey, CA 90241

Be sure to tell them what country you want your pen pal to be from. Also remember to include your full name, age, and address.

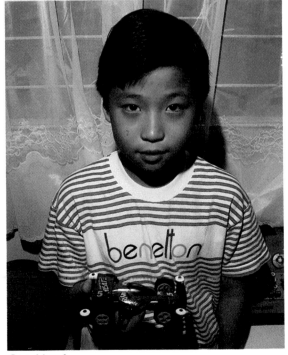

Good-bye!

Index